# INSTRUCTION MANUAL TO LIVE IN THIS NEW ERA

Keys to find happiness in a world that is collapsing around us

Ana Rodríguez

Copyright © 2014 Ana Rodríguez.
All rights reserved. This book or any part of it may not be reproduced or
used in any way without the express written permission of the publisher,
except for the use of brief quotes
or quotations in a review of the book.

Photos and drawings by Ana Rodríguez
First printing: 2014

ISBN: 978-1-291-76340-9

To the Mastermind that made it possible for this text to reach you

# What's in here?

What's in here?................................................................ v
What you will find in this book ................................... 7
In summary .................................................................... 9
1  Name yourself boss................................................. 11
2 Define your goal..................................................... 13
3 Learn how to talk ................................................... 19
4 Love and respect yourself ...................................... 25
5 Apply the golden rule ............................................ 29
6 Beware your thoughts, because YOUR THOUGHTS
   CREATE YOUR REALITY ................................... 31
7 The heart of the matter: feeling and emotion ..... 33
Think big: we can heal the whole world.................. 41
Bibliography ................................................................ 43
About the author ........................................................ 45
Other books by the author......................................... 47
Summary of the instructions..................................... 55

# What you will find in this book

Dear reader:

As we all know, life is made up of time and, for every second that passes, we have less and less of it.

On the other hand, things are not what they used to be. We just need to take a look around us—at the state of the economy, religion, politics and work, to name a few. Even the foundations of science, including medicine, which were unshakable for so long, are starting to crack too.

I have spent many hours researching and have come to the following conclusion: my time must be of the highest quality possible.

The question, then, would be: how can we improve the quality of our lives? Answer: with knowledge... first. Then, with experience. We just need to know what new rules this emerging world works under and apply them. It's that simple!

These new rules can be summarised as follows:

**MORE HEART & LESS BRAIN**

Don't worry: I will develop this idea a bit more in the shape of seven keys that have actually helped me a lot in living the life I truly want.

The decision to live a better life is yours and only yours. For a better life, some adjustments are required; for a worse life, all you need to do is nothing. Complaining and spending long hours on a solfa will not help you.

Great news! The historical moment we are living in right now makes change happen faster and more easily than ever before. This is the opportunity to invest our time in this new era.

If you consider yourself mediocre and are happy to lead a mediocre life, congratulations! Sit tight and spare yourself the trouble of reading any further. However, if you feel you deserve a change in your life (guess what: you deserve all the best—it's your birthright!), then you'll need to stand out from the crowd you've chosen to belong to and move towards the crowd you'd like to be part of.

If this is for you, then keep reading.

# In summary

To be concise, all instructions included in this manual could be summarised in just one statement—and that would be the end of the story:

However, I understand a travel guide would help a lot!

This manual is very easy to follow, understand and apply. I would have liked to write on a sphere, because all the information is interrelated. However, since two-dimensional writing is a lot more common, I have written the instructions one after the other.

Please, bear in mind that, due to the connection between them all, you'll notice how working on each one helps the others develop at the same time.

Without any further ado, let's dive into the promised instructions.

# 1 Name yourself boss

You are the boss of your life. You—and only you. Therefore, every aspect of your life is your responsibility.

Taking this into consideration, you have two options:

a) Complain and blame others

b) Face whatever the problem is and move your arse! (My apologies). In other words: take the ownership of EVERYTHING that happens to you.

Silence…

This is a fantastic moment for the head to start producing a long list of reasons (i.e., excuses) why you think a particular area in your life isn't working as smoothly as you'd like it to:

- I don't get promoted because I don't speak languages—but how could I, if I don't have any spare time to attend classes?

- In this crisis, there's absolutely no way to get a job; the ones to blame are:

a) the government

b) my parents

c) my spouse

d) my boss

e) all of the above

- If only I were younger/older I could tell a different story…

Just by repeating things to ourselves, we end up believing them! Listen: we become what we think.

One of my favourite excuses was the classic: "I don't have time". Of course, I have no time to paint my whole house inside and out every morning after breakfast. But I do have time to paint a ceiling one day and another one the next week or month.

Where to start?

Just keep reading.

# 2 Define your goal

A good boss makes use of their brain to organise a project and, of course, has a very clear image of what the final goal is.

How do you want each key aspect of your life to be: relationships, family, health (including weight), work, money, travel, dreams, spirituality, your relationship with yourself…?

Get a pen and some paper or a keyboard and screen or a tablet —whatever device you normally use—and start writing. Not in your mind! Write it down. In as much detail as you possibly can. Take your time—after all, you're writing the script of your own life. The only requirements are that you write in the present tense and that you are the leading actor. The more details, the better the script.

Going deeper into this idea: it's better to write a little every day, rather than pour loads of words in one go and then leave the whole project abandoned.

Perseverance. A grain at a time, you can move a whole mountain.

Remember: if you wish for a different life, you must do something you haven't done so far—because what you have been doing has led you to where you are now... And clearly, you wouldn't mind a change for the better.

Think of the huge amount of effort and time (i.e., life) we spend in things that do not really fulfil us—things we do only because we believe we ought to. Did you plan this kind of life? Do you think that this is what life is about, that there are no more options? That this is the price to pay for being alive? Did you take that job because there are so few? Do you think you have to swallow disrespectful comments from relatives, friends or workmates? Do you think luxuries and holidays are only for the (wicked) rich?

If that's the way you think, my congratulations! Congratulations, because you've got exactly what you created in your mind. You've made your dreams —or beliefs—come true.

By the way, are these beliefs truly yours? Or did you allow other to influence them, crisis included? The people you spend the most time with... what do they talk about?

The good news is that this is a reversible process. Plan differently and, little by little —although faster each time— you'll see how your life changes for the better.

Plan where you want to go. It's essential that you create our own future. Otherwise, you'll end up going around blindly, letting life lead you, instead of you steering life towards where you want it to go.

And if you decide to change your destination midway, no problem! The most important thing is to have a plan. And a BIG one!

Let's look at an example to help us get a clearer picture of this concept. Let's say what you love doing most, ever since you were a child, is playing the bagpipes.

To keep it simple, let's imagine the plan you came up with looks like this: Study Law, work as a lawyer to earn enough money to retire (at some point) and then, once retired, you'd finally have time for your beloved bagpipes. If you are lucky, this will happen before 67.

Now, let me tell you something: these days, only five out of a hundred retired people are financially free and only one out of a hundred has no financial shortages. On top of that, only one out of three people makes it past the age of 65. Hair-raising, isn't it?

Okay. Your schoolmate absolutely loved salsa dancing and dreamt of bringing his art to stages around the world. Today, he's earned more than enough to live without working and, more importantly, he is very, very happy. He keeps dancing… because that is what he wishes to do. Plus, how do you think his health is?

Which profile—and be sincere—do you identify with? I'll confess: I followed the first model for 25 years, if not more.

Statistics show that people who follow the second model tend to be more successful in life.

Let's take a look at some of these numbers. Back in 1979, interviewers asked new graduates from Harvard's MBA

Programme the following question: Have you set clear, written goals for your future and made plans to accomplish them? Here's what they found:

- 84% of them had no specific goals at all
- 13% had goals, but had never written them down
- 3% had clear goals, written down, with plans to accomplish them

Ten years later, the same graduates were interviewed again and the results were as follows:

- 13% of the students who had goals were earning, on average, twice as much as the 84% who had no goals
- The 3% who had clear goals and plans were earning, on average, ten times as much as the other 97% put together.

No comments. I know this survey only takes money into account and we know money does not bring happiness (although it helps!). But we all know how good it feels inside when we reach our goals, when we excel, when we push past the limits we think we have.

Once the goal is clearly defined, make a plan and focus on taking the first step. If your goal is to learn a new language, you might not have the resources for private tuition or to travel abroad for a few months. But you can definitely learn one world a day in that language, which adds up to over 300 a year. You can also spend a few minutes a week on the internet, where you can learn virtually everything for free. And if your excuse is you don't have a computer or internet access, go to a library! It's free!

Our part of the deal is to define the goal clearly—and take a step. Then, another step will follow… and another one, and another one and another one. How to eat an elephant? One mouthful at a time.

How the way will unfold ahead of us for us is unknown. But we don't need to worry about that. Things will happen—as simple as that. It's the universe's complimentary gift, on special offer right now. Time is on sale—everything is happening much faster.

How to define our goal or goals? With the use of words!

And yes… You guessed it right—you already know what the next step is.

# 3 Learn how to talk

Let's say our goal is to move from the XL size we're in at the moment to an L. Now, let's compare these two sentences:

- *I want to lose weight*

- *My weight is perfect. I feed my body with what it needs and it gets stronger and healthier every day*

Although the goal is the same—getting into a smaller size—the language we use to express it is completely different.

If I say to myself *I want to lose weight*, our subconscious mind assumes we are overweight because, otherwise, the sentence wouldn't make any sense.

Let me be insistent here: When we keep telling ourselves something, we end up believing it.

Now, think on the phrase *I need to lose weight*. How does it make you feel? Can you sense the weight of obligation… plus the load of guilt… and the of fat, probably heavier than it actually is?

In this regard, I strongly recommend *The Four Agreements*, by Dr Miguel Ruiz. The first of the agreements deals with the impeccability of your word.

Something that's really helped me has been listening to what successful people say—and how they say it—so I can copy it. Also, the other way around: listening to people who aren't successful and avoiding their sloppy habits has always been incredibly enlightening.

As children, we learn to speak through repetition. As grown-ups, we keep repeating what we hear. With that in mind, notice what your conversation topics are. If your only source of conversation is the media, perhaps it's time to consider adding something else to your life?

If we are a bit short on resources, what about copying success? When we were younger, that's something we'd do without blinking. Back then, our creativity was less polluted by other people's beliefs.

The media, people on the street and even those in our close circles often show us plenty of examples of how mediocre people talk. Their speech is full of low-energy words, such as: *crisis, corruption, greed, violence, economy, disease, fear, unemployment, limitation, shortage, riot, poverty*... Now, please compare this list with this one: *opportunity, challenge, change, love, empowerment, freedom, celebration, gratitude, growth, abundance, wealth, health*...

Please, do read again these two groups of words. Slowly. Pause on each one and pay attention to how you feel when you think of it.

Let's now take an example of high- and low-energy words we might use in our internal dialogue when facing a situation. In this case, the outcome of my very first Spanish omelette (*tortilla*, a word you must know!)... as you can see it in this photograph:

a) *What a crappy tortilla! It couldn't have come out worse! Besides... with vegetables! Silly me! My first attempt and I was foolish enough to add vegetables, as if just spuds, onion and egg weren't enough to start with! How stupid can you get? And... what a waste of money and time! Because no doubt it'll taste disgusting. Even if it didn't, it looks so awful no one will dare take a bite. Money straight to the bin. I already know how bad I am at cooking, I don't even know why I tried! I feel so embarrassed! I'm a failure. Anyone can cook a tortilla but me. My children will think I'm a bad mum because I'm such a failure in the kitchen...*

And on and on and on…

b) *Wow! Am I brave!? I had never cooked a tortilla before in my life, and I had the courage to start with not with a plain one but with one with added vegs! I'm going to send a picture to my friends—I'm sure it'll make them laugh! They might even volunteer to teach me how to make proper tortilla and we can have a great time together. The best thing about this is that I can only improve! My children can see that I've tried, I've done my best, and will witness the process of improving through practise. Also, if my tortillas don't get any better after some attempts, I could always move on to cakes. Plus, I'm pretty sure I'm one of the few people who have a picture of their first tortilla. I'm so happy I've faced my fear to be compared to my sister's… pieces of art!*

The fact is the same—but which character will feel better? What is character a) adding compared to character b)? Is it worth it to talk or think like a)? No brainer! If you think a) adds happiness and wellbeing to your life, get yourself checked out!

If we feed ourselves with texts, images and words that mostly carry grief, sorrow, violence, blame, resentment, fear and the like, what do you think will come out of us?

Mother Nature teaches me that cows poop grass because they feed on grass. She also teaches me that we always get apple trees from apple seeds… unless we water them with acid or bleach; in that case, we get nothing or very little.

We are born with the seed of grandeur. It's in our hands to help it grow to its full potential. If we feed a seed with what a plant naturally needs, it will grow as much as the size of the flowerpot allows and the amount of light it needs.

If you were born to be a sequoia… will you really resign yourself to be a bonsai?

Now, day after day—who do you talk to the most? Exactly! Yourself!

With that thought in mind, let's move on to the next instruction:

# 4 Love and respect yourself

It might be pretty useful to take a careful look at our internal dialogue and pay attention to those comments, attitudes and everyday behaviours that show very little affection towards ourselves. Here's an easy clue: what do I do for others that I do not do for myself? More clues: *What do I state about myself? Where do I set the boundary between what I deserve and what I don't? What do I feel bad about but always forgive others? What kind of life do I believe I deserve?* Let's be unbiased observers of how we treat ourselves—without judgment—and see what information we gather.

If we're hard on ourselves, how do you think we will treat others? Or maybe we are the type who seeks appreciation from others by playing the victim-poor me... (*Love me, for I've been abandoned/I'm old/I'm not healthy/I've been sacked*)?

Breaking the daily routine to include new habits might not be easy at first. Some say that, in order to create a habit—such as brushing our teeth before bed—we need to do this for 90 days in a row. After those 90 days, we'll keep doing it automatically, to the point we won't even consider going to bed with our teeth unbrushed, no matter how tired we are. But considering this new era brings opportunities with it, we can create new routines in far less time.

Well—if we've been able to insert around nine hours of work in our daily routines, doing something that doesn't always make us happy… And if we are also able to grab some time to watch the news and adverts on telly… Then, logic says it should be very easy to gather a few minutes—MINUTES—to be alone with our thoughts. Let's take that time to tell ourselves how well we've done this or that. To go over the marvellous things that happened to us during the day. To remind ourselves how beautiful we are. To think about how we've improved in dealing with things that used to make us explode like a grenade.

Giving yourself a massage, a beer, a trip, a scented candle, a walk, a bubble bath, a few minutes in silence—these are all ways of showing love and care to yourself.

Dare to think about what you wish for and give it to yourself.

Show respect to yourself by taking care of your body, your appearance, your posture. I find it hard to believe that someone dressing all scruffy, walking hunched over, with their gaze fixed on the ground could be the image of a person who truly loves themself. Let's model successful people—their attitude, the way the talk and walk, how firmly they shake hands, their facial expression, the light in their eyes, the energy they radiate…

For many people, giving is so much easier than receiving! However, a lack of coherence makes things unsustainable. If we give others all that we don't give to ourselves, resentment will eventually appear, whether in the form of a huge argument… or even in the form of illness.

From my point of view, the difference between instructions 3 and 4 becomes non-existent once we understand we are one.

Those surrounding us mirror what we are—or what we judge. In other words: what we simply do not accept… what we resist… what we hate.

Let's move into the next instruction:

# 5 Apply the golden rule

What's the Golden Rule? Treat others as you'd like them to treat you.

Have you ever screamed, in the middle of a big row, *would you like me to do the same to you?* And then, ten minutes later, we don't listen carefully when they talk to us. Or we criticise others. Or we shout or punish harshly when someone does something we don't agree with. Is that what we want for ourselves? To not be listened to? To be criticised behind our backs? To be shouted at? To be scorned when we did something in good faith?

Give what you wish to receive. If it is recognition, value the others; if it's love, love others; if it's money, donate. It also works the other way round. If you don't want to be criticised, offended or mistreated... stop doing it. If you're still receiving a kind of treatment you don't use on others, it's because you there's still a lesson to learn. You may still need to accept that part of yourself that's inflexible when dealing with certain issues. You need to learn to forgive what you judge, because we only reach peace by forgiving.

As we said before, we are surrounded by mirrors. We see in others what we love about ourselves and also what we judge. That is, those parts of ourselves we don't like much and don't want to accept as our own, because we label them *negative*. This is judgement: to consider things as good or bad.

I can't stand it when someone lies to my face and refuses to admit it, no matter what. But who suffers more? Me, ruminating it over and over? Or the other person, who will never admit their mistake and now has a reason to despise me?

My experience over the years shows me that, whenever I face a conflict, I can choose between being right… or having peace. If I choose peace, I must forgive—myself, the issue or the other person—in my heart. NB: with feeling. I must *feel* in my heart that I've forgiven them—the issue, myself or all of the above. I've also learned that I can use my freedom to choose who I want to be surrounded by—and who I'm better off leaving outside.

In the name of consistency, let's treat ourselves well. Expecting others to treat us in a way we *don't* treat ourselves doesn't make any sense. The wheel starts with us. It's better to consider ourselves good cooks, for instance—and prepare our dishes as best as we can—than to wait for others to tell us how good we are *before* we start believing it. Successful people sell themselves well, don't they?

See how important it is—what we think of ourselves? Now, let's take it one step further. How important do you think it is… what we think about EVERTHING?

# 6 Beware your thoughts, because <u>YOUR THOUGHTS CREATE YOUR REALITY</u>

(Can you tell I think this point is very, very important?).

What is a thought? It's our mental guidance, our potential—the idea that can set us get in motion. That is, of course, *if* we choose to act on it. If we simply fantasise about creating an opera we hear in our head but never get around to bringing it into the material world… it'll die with us.

As far as I know, our thoughts are the first step in creating our reality. As I mentioned before, we're living through a historic moment—a time when the materialisation of our ideas is faster and easier than ever. Remember? Yes—the opportunity this new era brings us!

There is no need to understand how something works to get advantage of it, just like we don't need to know how electrons move inside a hard drive to print off a document from our computer.

What is our 'reality'? Simply put, we could say our reality is what we want it to be. We receive information from our senses, but ultimately, it's our interpretation of this information that gives it meaning. Our mind processes what it gathers through the senses in the form of electrical impulses. And the mind sees what it *wants* to see, because it focuses its attention on whatever confirms what it has already decided to believe as true.

Let's say my eyes see a car runs over a cat. I relive the moment when, at ten, *my* cat was run over by a car and I was sad for a whole month. My reality today, at forty-eight, is that I spend the whole day in sadness, instead of a few seconds, like another person witnessing the same event might be sad. The long sadness becomes my reality—because it's my choice. I gather facts, pass them through my experience and make a decision.

If I think I am not lucky in love—with my romantic partners, for instance—I'll figure out ways to go through experiences that confirm that belief. It is called 'self-fulfilling prophecy'. *I told you so* is a favourite phrase of those suffering from the condition of seeing the glass half empty. They usually consider themselves 'realistic'.

Is it enough to think positively to make things happen? I believe that many readers and viewers of *The Secret* and many others who saw a glimpse of hope in the New Age movement got stuck on this idea and didn't dig into the heart of the matter: Step number seven of the present manual.

# 7 The heart of the matter: feeling and emotion

The powerful tool this new era brings us is precisely this: now, we now have access to the technology that allows us to define what we wish our lives to be like. In a few words: we can create our future and 'bring heaven to earth'.

Mankind split their mind from their heart—and this has led to the lack of coherence we live in today. Everything feels difficult. We fall ill. We search for answers in the wrong places. And yet... A flower knows perfectly when to bloom, without setting an alarm on its phone. Millions of animals migrate thousands of miles with no GPS whatsoever. A virus settles into a cell, even though it has no eyes, no weapons, no tools to see or conquer it.

Our mind judges; our heart sees and takes action. Our heart guides us taking into account the facts as they are: unbiased, without labelling them as good or bad. In other words, with no judgement.

Who's up for a change? More free time? Better health? Stronger relationships? More money? It's as simple as this: we choose what we wish and experience it with every part of us, as if those wishes had already been granted. Mastering these two things—clearly defining what we wish for and feeling it as though it's already ours—has been a long-life lesson for some souls... Yes: *at least* one lifetime. Once again: we're in opportunity time now!

At this moment in history, the Earth's magnetism is decreasing and its frequency is rising. These statements might mean nothing to you and that's okay. What matters is knowing that these two measurable parameters influence much of our cellular, genetic and emotional responses. Once again, we don't need to be experts in Geology, Physics, Quantum Physics, Astronomy, Astrology or even have our passports in date to activate the mechanism that produces one future or another.

What's happening right now is that the Universe is offering us a stronger connection—a kind of a broadband—that allows change to happen faster, thanks to those shifts in magnetism and frequency. By the way, these shifts are simply a reflection of what's happening on a larger scale. *As above, so below.*

I ☼ was taught to pray this way: by repeating prayers. I was told that praying was an act of glorifying God. Then, a new component was added before diving into the sport of repeating words: intention. If I didn't have a particular intention, I could always fall back on general ones: praying for those who were hungry, those in pain, those who suffer... But I was never invited to pray for anything joyful. Puzzling!

Here in the 21st century, I think I'm finally beginning to grasp the meaning of what I was *supposed* to understand back then. Maybe the words used weren't the most appropriate ones... Maybe my understanding wasn't yet able to pick up on the subtleties that were probably implied. Or maybe they simple didn't know what the deeper meaning of praying really was.

Let's say I now translate the paragraph marked with the sun ☼ like this: *Glorifying the divine intelligence through the feeling of gratitude. Being thankful for the food, care, health and wellbeing I enjoy. Feeling, deep inside, the peace I wish for myself and the whole world—a peace that I choose as my present, my past and my future.*

A bit different, hmm?

The key is the **emotion**. To truly feel the emotion—as if what we pray for were already here. In fact… it *is* true. We live in a field of infinite possibilities and we make real the ones we focus on, the ones we wish to become real.

It is not enough to think "I want a new car" and expect to find one as a prize in a cereal box. This is about imagining the new car as if it were already in the garage—seeing us in it, smelling the interior with our mind's eye, feeling the sun through the open roof, hearing the sound of the doors as they close and sensing the air moving through our hair (that's if we have hair, of course! ☺). It's about being fully convinced that this possibility is already here (breaking news: this possibility **is** here). It's about exuding gratitude through every corner and curve of our being. Not just the bits with or without a spare tyre around the middle… But also, the unseen ones—every layer of existence we currently occupy.

Furthermore, it's important to understand what's really behind our wish, because our mind might decide on something that's in contradiction with our feelings, with our heart. Let me insist once again: **coherence** is the fuel for this ancestral technology. If it's cracked, it does not work.

Dictionaries define 'feeling' and 'emotion' in very similar

ways. But in a holistic view of the world, we often speak of only two basic emotions: love and whatever we consider the opposite of love.

That opposite could be fear and it includes any mix of emotional states that disturb our inner peace, such as anger, jealousy, low self-esteem, rage and so on. We move through life driven by one of two forces: pleasure—which is self-explanatory—or fear.

Fear of what might happen if we make a particular decision. Fear of what others might think of us. Fear of the consequences. Fear of losing something. Better to stay as I am… than to step into the unknown.

A motor is a driving force. Our motors are love and fear.

I am going to use an example included in Gregg Braden's *The Isaiah Effect*. Braden sept several months collecting data. He asked the people attending his seminars what they prayed for. These are the main reasons, in order:

- To get more money
- To get a better job
- For good health
- To improve relationships

First: praying for more money, with no specification whatsoever on how much, when and what for… Well, that's something that's definitely not going to happen to us, because we've got it all clearly defined, right? ☺

When Braden asked the participants who were praying for more money to describe their thoughts about it, their answers fell into the following categories:

*I don't have enough.*

*I'm running out of it*

*I need more* and so on.

Clearly, these thoughts are associated with an emotion of fear. Braden then asked what feelings arose when combining the thought *I don't have enough* with the emotion of fear. He received a range of answers—from no answer at all to something like *I feel very bad.* No wonder! Who could feel good in that state? Look at this: the concatenation 'thought-emotion-feeling' becomes:

more money → fear → I feel very bad

How the hell are we supposed to make more money… if we're doomed to feel crap about it?

So, the question is: How can we change this connection between money and feeling bad? The answer is: by changing the words that express our thoughts, by bringing the idea of <u>love</u> into it. That means choosing words that align with life and that summon peace.

Here is a made up example about money:

*I wish to have a passive income that keeps growing month after month over the next year until it gets to €5,000 per month. The money flows to me effortlessly, with joy, in peace and harmony with the rest of the world. It allows me to go on holidays twice a year wherever I wish. It also allows me to help the people I love, open my internet handcrafts business, attend international gatherings and free myself from domestic chores. It gives me more time to walk by the sea, invite my parents to take that trip to Egypt they've always dreamed of and invest part of my income, so it grows, so money works for me.*

I invite you to do this exercise with your own wishes and, please, let me know how it makes you feel. I think it's important to turn the mind off as much as possible, because it can easily interfere with questions like *€3,000 in such a short period of time? And as passive income? Impossible!* It's only impossible if we think it's impossible. Never place limits on your wishes! Think BIG, for God's sake!

In fact, the amount of money I have used in the example—whether euros, dollars, pounds or whatever currency of a similar magnitude—is ridiculously low. Why? Because I know what happens to the mind when it sees too many zeros: It short-circuits! It just can't handle them. But don't worry—we can start small. Adding zeros along the way will happen smoothly and naturally.

For me, this is what prayer is: Feeling that I already enjoy what I wish for, feeling grateful for it, letting myself sink into the emotion of peace and love that comes from that wish being real. That wish—that truth—already exists in reality. It's already here—I just might not see it yet because I'm too focused on other realities.

So far, I've talked about the instructions we can apply to ourselves, because it's within us that we have the power to begin making the necessary adjustments to get the outcome we're looking for. At the very least, we can start here. Let's keep in mind, though, that we are cells within a greater organism: humankind. Part of an even bigger one: the Earth, which belongs to a galaxy, one among millions in the Universe. And the Universe? One among… who knows how many. On the other hand, our own bodies are made up of cells. Each one feels, thinks and interacts with its environment. Each one is formed by protein chains, molecules, atoms, particles…

Our thoughts modify our biochemistry, our cells, our DNA. Likewise, these changes affect in the bigger scale.

Taking this into consideration, how far can our prayers and thoughts reach? Yes: the limit is… our imagination. So, how important do you think the *quality* of the thoughts we produce in our mental factory is?

# Think big: we can heal the whole world

What kind of world do we want to live in? A world where the media show us—because it seems to sell more—dead bodies, misfortune, abuse, robbery, scarcity, nonsense? Or do we prefer the Garden of Eden?

Our ancestors left us proof that this garden existed, our own Shargri-La: a world where human beings lived in complete harmony with Nature and were moved by love.

We have a window of opportunity to go back to Eden. How? By praying together—understanding prayer as the intention to choose one specific probability (peace, love, abundance, creativity, wisdom…) from the field of infinite possibilities; feeling it with all our being and adding gratitude as the star ingredient. Since we are all one, there is no limit whatsoever! We can receive whatever we wish to receive!

As for what else you can do as an individual, I invite you to look within yourself and find your talent, that is, if you still don't know what it is that makes you special and unique. I suggest you work on that talent until you master it. And then, use it to serve others; share it with them. That way, you'll be happy and will make others happy too.

If this last paragraph felt a bit alien to you, ask yourself the following questions:

- Is your work fulfilling or is it just a job?
- Would you still do it if you weren't paid for it?
- Does it free you… or enslave you?
- Would you be happy to keep it for the rest of your life or does it feel more like a life sentence?
- Do you have fun?
- Does time fly when you're doing it?
- Do you mind doing it on weekends?

When we are happy—when we enjoy ourselves—laughter is usually present. And laughter is contagious.

Without digging into the physics, metaphysics or biochemistry of why this is so, just bear in mind: you can access the Garden of Eden simply by practising the art of laughter. And this extends to everyone you *infect* with it. Therefore,

# Laugh a lot! ☺

# Bibliography

- *The Four Agreements,* Dr. Miguel Ruiz, 2002.

- *Why 3% of Harvard MBAs make ten times as much as the other 97% combined,* Sidsivara.com.

- *What they don't teach you at Harvard Business School: notes from a Street-Smart Executive,* Mark. H. McCormack, 1986.

- *Awakening to Zero Point, the video,* Gregg Braden, 1997.

- *The Isaiah Effect: decoding the lost science of prayer and prophecy ,* Gregg Braden, 2001.

- *The Biology of Belief: Unleashing the power of consciousness, matter & miracles,* Dr. Bruce H. Lipton (2008).

- *A Course in Miracles,* Helen Shucman and William Thetford.

# About the author

I've dreamed of writing books since I was a little girl. But, like many, I was taught that the *winning formula* for life was to study hard, get a degree and secure a stable job until retirement. And so, I followed the script. Since scientific degrees were seen as more practical, I became a chemist and spent 20 years working for a salary.

Yet, deep inside, I kept asking myself: *What will I regret most when I retire—the moment I've been told I can finally start living?* The answer was always the same: I would regret not making space for my dreams. I would regret not owning my time. I would regret letting others decide my path. I would regret not being present for the people I love.

So, I took a leap of faith. I left behind a successful career to follow what my heart truly longed for—to pursue a happiness that always seemed just out of reach while I was chasing someone else's definition of success.

It hasn't been a straight road. I still spend time making money, but now, I do it more efficiently, freeing up space to follow my true calling. Each day, I shift the balance—less time earning a living, more time truly *living*.

Through trial and error, I've discovered that my greatest fulfillment comes from listening to my intuition and acting on it. When I do, life flows. I am happier. And so are the people around me.

And now, what my heart tells me to do is **share**—to pass on what I've learned and continue to learn every single day. So be it!

In the media, find me as Empowered Supernova.

# Other books by the author

This is the link in which you can find all my books on https://linktr.ee/Empowered.Supernova. I will continue updating the new titles there.

At the moment of publishing this book, these are the books that are already available in the English language:

# Empowerment books

*My first million: A spiritual and material approach to the noble art of making money*

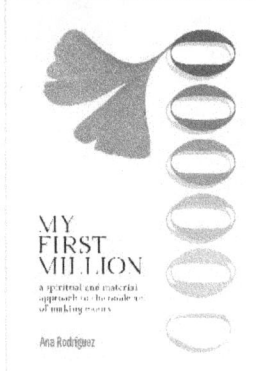 

https://tinyurl.com/MFM-BeB-Amz

*Empowered: Wealth, Health and You. Conquer the three and become the super version of you*

https://tinyurl.com/EmpoweredSuperYou-Amz

*The story I never wanted to tell: Farewell to marriage in peace and harmony*

https://tinyurl.com/TheStoryEN-Amz

*Instruction manual to live in this new era: Keys to find happiness in a world that is collapsing around us*

https://tinyurl.com/Insmanual-EN-Amz

*Konversations with my kids: Keys to build extraordinary relationships with your teenagers*

http://tinyurl.com/KonversationsEn1

*Konversations with my kids: The six human needs*

https://tinyurl.com/Konversations-En2

*Narcissistic mother: goodbye! Three steps to stop living under the shadow of the woman who believes she owns you*

## Children's books

*Halloween: Palabras - Words*

https://tinyurl.com/HalloweenPW-ENus-Amz

*Fun, feelings and emotions*

https://tinyurl.com/FFE-EN-Amz

*Hoppity Hopes and the unknown treasure*

https://tinyurl.com/Hoppity-EN-Amz

*Rhymes and riddles, giggles and tickles, Vol II*

https://tinyurl.com/Rhymes-II-EN

*Things you can do with your mouth*

https://tinyurl.com/Mouth-EN-Amz

# Summary of the instructions

### 1. Make yourself responsible for all your circumstances

Don't you dare complain about anything. You either have excuses or get results.

### 2. Define exactly what your goals are

Write them down in as much detail as possible. Then start working towards them immediately.

### 3. Mind your words

Speak positively, always aiming to uplift. Use high-vibration words.

### 4. Love and respect yourself

Be kind to yourself. Treat yourself. Feel good of your achievements. Love your body and soul… Every bit of you.

### 5. Apply the golden rule

Life is a boomerang: What you give is what you receive.

### 6. Mind your thoughts!

What surrounds you is the direct result of your past thoughts. Step one to get different results: think differently.

### 7. Live your wishes with all your being

Feel deep gratitude as if it has already been granted.

Find your talent or talents.
Share them.
Be the best version of yourself.
And, overall,

## ☺ Laugh a lot! ☺

www.ingramcontent.com/pod-product-compliance
Lightning Source LLC
Chambersburg PA
CBHW031431040426
42444CB00006B/765